GW01454523

VICTORIA PRIMARY SCHOOL

3

"Inspired by my sons Dan and Jordan,
City fans who kept believing,
and driven by Mick a fellow believer"
Jamie

Sara, Laura and Dan
"We made history"
Dad

Written by Mark Graham
Illustrated by Rob Palmer

Based on an idea by Jamie Fletcher
Produced by Mick Shackleton

Special thanks to Phil Abbott, Paul Firth, Mark Neale and Lisa Barr

First published by FoBCFC in 2013
Friends of Bradford City
BD13 2BL

www.friendsofbcfc.co.uk

Copyright © Friends of Bradford City 2013

ISBN 978-0-9927226-0-9
All rights reserved
Printed in the United Kingdom

THE League OF DREAMS

Endorsed by Bradford City

Jimmy was a small boy with a big dream.
He wanted to play football at Wembley Stadium.
Jimmy was football daft!
When he wasn't playing football in the garden
or talking to his friends about football,
he was watching football on the telly.

Jimmy soon grew from being a small boy
into a really tall young man.
He left school and got a job
working at the Co-op.
Being the tallest meant that he could reach the things
on the highest shelves that nobody else could.
Jimmy liked his job, but he hadn't forgotten his dream.

Sometimes, you need a little bit of luck
to help a dream come true
and today was Jimmy's lucky day.
He was playing for his local team
when a man came to watch.
Later that evening, Jimmy got a phone call.
Would he like to play for Bradford City?

Of course he would!
Now Jimmy was a proper footballer.
But it was hard work.
City were going through a bad time
and losing too many matches.
His dream of playing at Wembley
still seemed a long way off.

When the new season started,
there was a real buzz about the place.
Jimmy met some old friends and lots of new faces at the club.

Gary, Andrew, Nathan, Nahki and Rory were there.
Mr Parkinson the manager
gathered Jimmy and the other players around.
"If we believe in each other," he said,
"we can make our dreams come true!"

The trouble was,
all the other teams were dreaming
that it would be THEIR big season too.
After Christmas, City started to struggle.
When they lost to Oxford,
the club mascot Billy Bantam
saw that Jimmy was disappointed.
"Chin up Jimmy," he said,
"never stop believing!"

T&A
COUNTY DEFEATED IN EXTRA TIME

T&A
WATFORD BRUSHED ASIDE

SPORT NEWS
PREMIERSHIP WIGAN BEATEN ON PENALTIES

NEWS UPDATE
CITY GIANT KILLERS

SPORT NEWS
A CITY DARES TO DREAM

WORLD NEWS
CITY HEROES DEFEAT ARSENAL

WHAT AN AMAZING NIGHT!

SPORT
LEAGUE CUP

BRADFORD 3 - 2 ARSENAL
LATEST FROM VALLEY PARADE   After Penalties

UNBELIEVABLE JEFF!

GOAL!

With things not going too well,
City were pleased to have some cup games too.

In the first round they beat Notts County!
Next, in the second round, they beat Watford!
After that, in the third round, they beat Burton!
Two weeks later, in the fourth round, they beat Wigan!
Then, in the fifth round, they beat the mighty Arsenal!

City were so close to Wembley!
In the semi-final, Nahki scored
and City beat Aston Villa 3-1 at home.
But they still had to play another game at Villa's ground.
Nobody expected City to win.
Villa scored an early goal.
Now City were only winning 3-2,
but then they got a corner.

Jimmy jumped...

GOAL!

22

...and thumped a great header into the top corner!
GOAL!
The fans went wild and as Jimmy ran towards them,
he knew that his dream was about to come true.
Villa scored again but it was too late.
The final whistle went and Jimmy and Bradford City
were going to Wembley!

But dreams don't always turn out as we hope
and sadly for Jimmy,
this one turned into a nightmare.
The City players were nervous
and lost the final by a whopping five goals to nil.
Jimmy was upset,
but he still remembered Billy Bantam's wise words,
"Never stop believing!"

YORKSHIRE

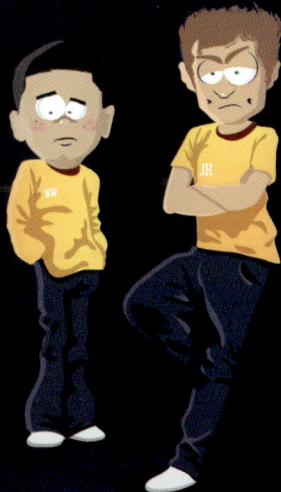

City might just have a second chance.
If they could do well in their last few games,
they could still make it to the play-off final.
With one big effort, Jimmy and his team mates did it!
They were going back to Wembley.

BRADFORD CITY
TEAM COACH

LONDON

Because they had played at Wembley before,
the City players weren't so nervous this time.
Jimmy scored another fantastic header
and it was City's turn to win easily.
As Jimmy waved to the cheering fans,
he knew that sometimes dreams really can come true
if you work hard and never stop believing.

29